THE
COURT
OF
NO
RECORD

JENNY MOLBERG

POEMS

THE
COURT
OF
NO
RECORD

LOUISIANA STATE UNIVERSITY PRESS   BATON ROUGE

Published by Louisiana State University Press
lsupress.org

Copyright © 2023 by Jenny Molberg

LSU Press Paperback Original

DESIGNER: Barbara Neely Bourgoyne
TYPEFACE: Adobe Caslon Pro

Cover illustration courtesy Shutterstock.

Library of Congress Cataloging-in-Publication Data
Names: Molberg, Jenny, 1985– author.
Title: The court of no record : poems / Jenny Molberg.
Description: Baton Rouge : Louisiana State University Press, [2023]
Identifiers: LCCN 2022031744 (print) | LCCN 2022031745 (ebook) |
    ISBN 978-0-8071-7902-4 (paperback) | ISBN 978-0-8071-7972-7 (pdf) |
    ISBN 978-0-8071-7971-0 (epub)
Subjects: LCGFT: Poetry.
Classification: LCC PS3613.O445 C68 2023 (print) | LCC PS3613.O445
    (ebook) | DDC 811/.6—dc23/eng/20220707
LC record available at https://lccn.loc.gov/2022031744
LC ebook record available at https://lccn.loc.gov/2022031745

FOR PUJA

There can be no love without justice.

—bell hooks, *All About Love*

CONTENTS

3. WHAT LOVE DOES

THE
COURT
OF
NO
RECORD

MAY THE STARS GUIDE YOU SAFELY HOME

After I call the cops to ask for a protective order
I read about the girlfriend of a serial killer. What she knew,

what she didn't. How it seems we're always punished
for asking questions. America is watching a show

about a man who is fascinating. His eyes ice
behind the fog of his glasses.

Such a nice guy. Such a quiet guy. The flooded house.
I don't care about him. I want to say their names:

Ann Bryan. Katherine Ann Hall.
Hardee Schmidt. Joyce Williams.

Lillian Robinson. Marilyn Nevils.
Johnnie Mae Williams. Donna Bennett Johnston.

When I call the cops
I hold my arm like a seatbelt. When I call the cops

a woman answers. Hand over chest like an elementary
school lie: the pledge, the flag, the wrong math.

The girlfriend rode in the car and didn't know
about the woman in his trunk. Not two people there,

but three. When I call the cops the officer speaks like an aunt,
Honey, don't you know this only makes it worse?

The law provokes, a split tongue made of amendments.
As a child I used to dream

of walking down my city street, past the newspaper
stand, to our corner house with its porthole window,

the garage that spilled open like a mouth. I'd ring
the doorbell and another mother would answer, her children

like impressions of me. I thought I lived there.
The system is turning me to sand.

Honey, if I were you I'd sit tight, get a gun. The killer's girlfriend
killed a man once. The author of the book about the killer

says she liked the feeling of being desired.
He might as well say she was asking for it.

A biker in a Sons of Silence jacket broke a pool cue
over the girlfriend's back so she fought and then she was fighting

not a man but an idea, not one thing but many,
and then the man was dead. She carried

his photo in her wallet for years. We're watching the show
of America because we want to win.

To win means kill and not be killed.
This helps the system. The court believes the bad actor.

Before I call the cops I call a domestic abuse advocacy center.
They say *conflict of interest.* They say *he got there first.*

I try to say it's all backwards.
I try to say please listen to me.

The night of the hearing I awake thinking
I am the girlfriend, the silence of the trunk

an ocean. It takes hours to rise, to gather myself,
part by part, pulling the truth from the dark.

This is my face. This is my name.
Someone loves me.

My voice is animal in the courtroom microphone.
Behind the judge, the sideways prison of the flag.

1.

EXPECTING

This is a case without a body.
The body does not come into it at all.

—SYLVIA PLATH, "The Detective"

THE PINK BATHROOM

> Rose Fishman, found dead in her home, March 31, 1942:
> a crime scene constructed by Frances Glessner Lee,
> an investigation training exercise for detectives.

Rose Fishman is a doll.
Rose Fishman is the reflection of a doll
in the pink bathroom's mirror.
Rose Fishman is dressed like an old woman
in the pink bathroom's mirror.
Rose Fishman hated her old womanness
so ended it. Or Rose Fishman was ended by a man
because a man hates the girls of his mind,
his own mother reflected in the injured glass.
Why must she be a mirror? He wants you
to look at his hate through her eyes in the mirror.

Rose Fishman is just a doll
dressed like an old woman
painted to look like she is dead.

        burnt umber for the purge fluids
        pointillismed with the smallest paintbrush
        under the fishbowl of a magnifying glass
        the cloth body the robe an envelope
        the tangle of the doll's triangled arms
        extra stuffing for ankle bloat
        black hair askew the eyes can't see

Rose Fishman is captured
in the pink bathroom,
cops mooning their pearly cheeks
over the surface of her privacy.

pink crinoline curtains pink tiebacks
the round pink rug a fringed bandage
salmon marbled sink
and the mirror and Rose in the mirror
roses and fish repeating until everything is ripcurl
ripcurl of roses and fish in the vanity mirror
the sink mirror door mirror and through the closed window
the waves pound their whitening fists

This is the whirlpool of self-hate:
Rose Fishman in her standstill age,
the cops studying women
like painted relics, ogling through glass,
their distorted fish eyes: hundreds, blinking.

Rose Fishman cared about her slippers.
Rose Fishman perfectly folded her pink towels.
Rose Fishman was found this way
by the doorman, her mail collecting dust,
her powder puff, her doilies, her pink fishbowl.
(The real Rose Fishman hated doilies. Let us honor the facts.)
Rose Fishman wore a blue robe.
Rose Fishman was neither rose nor fish
was the water so Rose Fishman is everywhere.

SHOOTING AT OAKBROOK APARTMENTS

My neighbor held a gun to his own chest
and with the other hand, his son,

captive for being his son. The bullet
punctured the man, the window, then the air

above my head as I peered over the fence.
A bullet to the chest can miss the heart.

Square in their studded epaulets and pressed
blue trousers, the officers did not call for backup,

puzzling under the apartment, walkie-talkies
staticking like wasps from their hips.

Luck is the brain's way of fooling yourself.
My neighbor lived. His son lived. The mother,

beating against the bathroom door, lived.
The cops left in their boats for the glutted swamp.

No passive voice—breeze taped out of a window's hole
My neighbor was making a choice.

Even then I knew I would never give birth.

BATON ROUGE, HARVEST MOON

Puts me in mind of C.
Whiskey on the pickup bed, 5 a.m., sky an oil spill.
After the storm we never went to bed.
Our street: blown-out billboards, emergency highway.
I went to meet the truck of animals, to try to help
in some way, but when the truck arrived
all the animals were dead.
Pulled from the mud for nothing.
I have never talked about the stain on the street
I drove past every day, where a car hit my friend.
Two green mallards fanned their wings
across C.'s back, one for each of his brothers.
The first was an accident. The second, grief.
I loved him in my dumb way.
When he passed out in the neighbors' trash
I lifted him, his black curls against my neck.
We had coffee but there was still whiskey in it.
His parents lived in the FEMA trailer
parked at the horse farm. They'd lost
their hardware store in Houma, the coast's eye.
Grief came up out of the earth.
There were many false saviors
with boats full of dogs. *Don't they know*
you can't build a grave in the swamp?
C. was the last brother. In the storm, the other two
rose out of the earth. He never talked to anyone.
I know nothing about loss. The prism of his face
at 5 a.m. was a question. What was left of the family
stood on the coast as the boats resurfaced.

INITIATION IN WHITE

dressed in thongs
we danced for the boys
who catcalled
from their folding chairs
drooling beer

be pretty like a polo horse
like a breast-patch of want
we stayed up all night

the girls blindfolded me
I walked parting curtains
of Spanish moss
until it was my own hair
& the night my face
they chanted my name
I went looking for myself

the night hot as underwear
don't let us see you dance with her again
don't make us look like lesbians
what I could not say is
what the boys do
what the boys had done

some of the girls circled your fat
some of the girls climbed into coffins
reborn as owls

the lake creeped closer
to the big plantation house
in the lake tails & gills

& maybe also girls
all the new girls wore white
southern angels
descending upon fate
as one does wearing white

a death an ending & the sheets we wore
billowed in the hot wind
broken birds
when they took off the blindfold
my eyes sweat in the black light
fuzzy with candles
two women held my hands
one was my mother
one was my grandmother
a circle of hoaxes

we three held on
our eyes brown & smudged
the jeweled key pinned to my heart
glittered a fish on the surface of me

the night so heavy it sat on your face
& I wanted that
& I wanted out
hundreds of same-girls in white
calling my name underwater
I willed myself
& left the dead of me

OCCAM'S RAZOR

My friend and I are trauma bonded.
When our abuser's wife lies, our Pegasus brains

blink on in the night, imaginary beacons.
If you hear hooves, remember: there are no unicorns,

only the meat-packing plant. The train you hear
is no tornado. Not northern lights,

but the sky's explainable chemistry.
Wittgenstein says, "If a sign is not necessary then it is meaningless."

The abominable snowman shoves one giant fur toe
beyond the tree line, testing our boundaries.

Swinburne says, "Either science is irrational or the principle
of simplicity is a fundamental synthetic a priori truth."

A woman's cop husband shot her twice in the head,
placed his service gun beneath her pajamaed chest.

Her fuzzy pink slippers peeked from the closet
The dog's leash a golden lasso on the floor.

A plurality can't be posited without meaning.
The cop husband invented his wife's suicide note,

thinking her dead. If you can sail around the world
then it is not flat. Our abuser's wife feeds the cat,

makes some calls, bandages her hand.
He says to her: don't push it.

We know why she lies. We lied for him too.

RUNAWAY

I make imaginary places where real things happen.
Caves filled with mangoes, a shop with misshapen dresses
covered in stains—people I love dead because I dreamed it.
Last night, it was my father and my mother could not cry
because her crying made it real. Friday night, the paws
of a neighborhood dog are left severed on my porch.
I feel what is missing of the dog until I am only hands and feet.
Fear catches like a bark in the throat. A man I know
wrote a book about a girl who took her own life.
He morphed himself into her, as if that could ever be
possible, which of course is an act of violence. What do I know,
writing my way out of fear. I used to pack a suitcase
full of candy and run away, pedaling down the street
while my mom shouted from the stoop. Pumping my hairy little legs
just to prove I could disappear. I once hid in the neighbor's
garage for hours beside an old Firebird that lived under a tarp.
It was the '80s. Satanic Panic. Stranger Danger. I watched my mother
grow afraid, the thrill of her panic inside me. It was real.
Having scared myself into grief, I went home.
She loved me like a mother, which of course
is an act of the imagination.

FAMILY WITH DREAMS CUT OUT

after Bridget Lowe

The dream is not the anger, real as a dream, but what I did with it.

The dream is the only way in. The dream is I am my father.

The dream is I am not. Counting as I wash my hands

the fifth, sixth, the seventh time. I want to be kind.

The dream is cruel as my mind is cruel in its fear of cruelty.

As the oldest child the dream was that I was neither

the mother nor the father. But I kept losing my children.

We left town. We forgot to remember our brother.

Then the sister left too, ingested by the sky as a dying storm.

The dream is a childhood levitation.

I rose, I started the car, I knew the hospital route by heart.

COLLISIONS

after C.D. Wright

The year they caught the first serial killer but not the second I lived with a woman who because of religion had only the most dangerous sex with men—I kissed her in the parking lot—brilliant, tall—she burned a hole through the rented carpet Someone followed her to work Drew smiley faces on all the menus She always felt someone was watching—locked doors twice—this was the year we drove down Magnolia Street hot-boxing the car Nutria dissolved into lakes Facts we could not know but felt The backs of our necks on fire I taught at the parish school My bag full of snack-packs Dahlia with her purple glasses her made-up words Jackson in his Batman suit Their lives waterbirds in my hands Julia's stepdad pulled her out of class His face closed as a box My roommate bled on the floor She wouldn't let me see it She walked home—night, indigo—a car parked outside shone its brights through the slatted blinds The man had followed her for weeks His teeth wet in the parking lot light—his eyes binoculars— he turned the wheel so the light covered our legs The cops never found him—they hardly found anyone—she rushed around the house turning over her pictures with men I didn't understand At school Julia wore a daisy-covered shirt When she came back to class we ignored our lesson sat in the corner—yellow plastic chairs—he kept hitting my mom she was saying I couldn't let it happen anymore The man not her father The blade in her hands—a line in the sand—I believed I knew what she meant but I've never been brave The flags from the belltower whipped The floors sticky everywhere I went All the ways I saw it didn't happen to me—then it did—

TRIGGER

Small rifle in my shoulder-crook, paper target
like a cartoon hallucination, the deer blinds,

my child-hand scattering the red clover & chicory,
believing in forgiveness. At 18 a man
held a gun to my head. At 22 another man opened

his car door & pointed as I threw myself in reverse.

BRIDGE

Ann Bryan, 1911–1994. Murdered, St. James Place
Retirement Community, Baton Rouge.

The women take their places at the bridge table,
this day without Ann. North, West, East.

I study Ann's black hair, a curled wreath, in the book
about her killer. Her large glasses exalt the kind

of eyes that speak. What right do I have
to think about Ann? Her painting

of a magnolia—the carpels, red and yellow
anemones cradled in a bed of white petal-spoons.

She is the killer's first victim. Small like the others:
her sewing kit, her purple quilt, the portable wooden floor

where she danced Zydeco. Why wouldn't I think
of my own grandmother? Ann, born without a right hand,

brushing light with paint on her blue still-life bowl
A hand that danced the whole keyed black-and-white road.

My grandmother's hands: arthritic, manicured, always
fisted. In bridge, my grandmother plays South.

My grandmother is the Declarer. She will give
until all that is left is her body.

When her son, my uncle, says she is selfish,
that his mess of a life is her fault, she believes him.

Once he bought a car with her money
and gave me my first lesson in threat.

I was twelve. I sat pretty. Kept all his secrets
while he drove, vodka balanced between his knees.

I rehearsed my praise,
how handsome he was, how rich.

Ann, I am sorry. There is no way
to elegize a person you don't know.

I can't even save my own grandmother.
But I have to try.

EXPECTING

The basement drain gurgles & the wind knocks
the window & the barn owl's face is treed.

I consume pears, cheese, stories about murder.
In the bayou, the engorged sun crowns in morning.

I piggyback a sweaty child. I try not to parent
kids who are not mine, but they live in our house,

they wake me at night, they want a story
in my best impression of a French au pair.

With my true-crime knowledge, I trim the hedges.
This is where the night stalker hides.

I carry the wood axe to the shed,
its stumped blade like too much aftermath.

I want love & not fear but these are the same.
The giant bridge over the Mississippi frowns

toward the city where once a woman told me
she'd end her life. Then she vanished in the night

wearing my name. My sister lies awake, recording sputters
that drum her belly like two bagged birds.

These days I want to sleep, really sleep, with the window
thrown open. I want to meet my sister's son.

ATTIC

Miss Jessie Comptom, found dead Tuesday, December 24, 1946:
a crime scene constructed by Frances Glessner Lee, an investigation
training exercise for detectives.

Yes, I listened to the records,
read the old letters in the box.

        The dead never get any privacy
        once they are bodies like me.

My humiliation teeters above the chair
in the attic so yes it lives on earth.

        Yes, I hung the laundry on the ceiling
        because it was raining and yes

I was thinking of the miller's
daughter but never the bad golden man—

        Yes he said he loved me, so what.
        He lives in Buffalo with his real family.

Yes I am dressed as a grandmother.
Yes, a costume: the shawl, the gray bun.

        Yes I am old but I don't think
        you know what that means.

I know how to tie a knot.
I spent many good days sailing. Still do.

        Yes one of my shoes was found on the stairs.
        Yes my other shoe dangles from my cotton ankle.

Shoes cannot fly.
A person cannot be killed alone.

      I won't tell you who did this to me.
      I am not talking to you

except through my body
which I give you to decode.

THE MINIATURIST

for Frances Glessner Lee

> . . . within within within.
> —SUSAN STEWART, *On Longing*

Cops in their badges and high-and-tight haircuts
squat to peer inside her dollhouse. She wants them to.
She wants them to see the overturned chair, white knit bear
the size of a child's toe. She teaches them to read a body.
Cigarettes rolled with receipt paper. The kiss of pink
on the underside of a pillow. A clue. What do you expect
her to hate about herself? I think I see Frances,
large hands under a jeweler's loupe, screwing a toothpick
into a weather vane. Yarning a sewing wheel.
Making dead women smaller so she can save them.
She stretches linoleum across her little kitchen. It's 1947.
She destroys what is painstaking. Blowtorches the roof.
Plants a bottle of Seconal. The pharmacist's name
small as a line of ants. Tuft of Siberian weasel in the ferrule
of her paintbrush. *I am a mirror as I rest beneath her gravestone,*
the biographer writes. *I must hate the woman they keep telling me to be,*
I think, peering into Frances, *so I can become what I might be.*
I am defusing. There is a fuse in me in the shape of a brush.
Stop making me sexual. Stop calling me *mine.*
My quilt is edged in rickrack. My glass of whiskey
a thimble full of sap. Pet milk in little cans on the sill.
I wake in the red bedroom with bangles on my wrists
and the old thought creeps in again.
I do not recognize my life. I do not recognize
these small woven socks, my gauzy nightgown,

my hands that move like mittens. There is blood on my clothes
and in my hair. No, it is nail polish. My windows
are plastic. My hands are in my hair. The noose
is made of cooking twine. A man is looking in.

HUNTING

The bow is an extension of the arm. The yellow-headed

blackbird knows to stop its singing. The gun is an extension

of the brain. A cow lows in the twilit field; the man says

she's looking for her calf. The elk heads line the wall.

The children have their mother's shot. The knife

is an extension of the hand. Find the place between

the ribs, he says. *Upward.* The hook is the extension

of the line. Bait is a human lie made with a fly-shaped mold.

Meat is the moment of death. Gun is the language that means

America. The bullet is an extension of the gun's idea,

which was a man's, a man who thought *all the way through.*

MY SCORPION

She coils her tail around my wrist, whispers me fire,
the blue part, the part that really breathes.

From the plaintiff table the lawyer asks *yes or no,*
yes or no. But none of the questions

are yes or no questions. The court clerk cleans his glasses
with his shirt. The man says the word again.

With a twang. A hard *r.* The obvious poplars
sprawl their umbrellas over the court of no record.

Nature. The man's anger rises beneath the table until
he must excuse himself. My scorpion is able to speak

and not speak. Her exoskeleton purples. No one touches her.
His reddening mouth. I wish everyone could see it like us.

Once I told the man on the other side
I didn't want to live anymore. Black smoke rose.

There was no other way out. My scorpion wears
the cold shadows. I used to trust my mind.

Then she appeared in autumn, armored, impossible.
I cannot say more about the man. The law is bone lonely.

The day my scorpion arrived I was rising. I cradle
my stinger. I carry her in my claw like an ache.

A JOKE

I walk with my friend into an antique store.
Two men stand by a Victrola, one in camouflage,
one in overalls. They drag their eyes over our bodies.
The one in overalls leans against a display of dead instruments
and I begin to understand the possibilities of my skin.
The fact of his knife in the belt loop.
The it of me tolls in my head. *Come here,* he says,
come here, he says. Some men like to put their hands
around your neck when they fuck you.
A little joke about murder, a little game of power.

            In a dream my partner poses
for a family portrait in my house with the woman who used to be
his wife. I am teaching his daughter to read. In the bedroom mirror
the place where my eyes should be is nothing. I see only
shades and shadows. Skin.

            The man in the camouflage
and the one in the overalls examine a pair of dolls
with straw that dangles from their mouths.
They are supposed to be Tom and Huck, faces
dotted with orange freckles. Tom doll wears whitewash
all over his pants. *Farm murder brothers,* my friend says to me.

            In the dream with no eyes
I go to a marketplace. A man takes me into his tent.
He closes the flaps. He takes his box of tools. He aims
his box cutter at the skin of my neck. He does not have to try
very hard. It does whatever it is told, this thing that can separate
me from my body. The joke is that I do not really live
in this body. When I turn the knife on him, his eyes go, too.

Two women with skin for eyes
walk into a bar. They see only shades or shadows.
One of them whispers her joke in the other's ear.
This is a game of overalls. A joke about power.

Two men walk into a bar.
Everyone orders chicken wings and wine.
My friend stands before me baring her teeth.
Two men live inside my mind as one monster.
I read true crime to learn escape. Inside the chest
of the monster lives the punch line: *I can make you love me.*

THE LIVING ROOM

Mrs. Ruby Davis, found dead in her home, May 22, 1941:
a crime scene constructed by Frances Glessner Lee,
an investigation training exercise for detectives.

The man has his drink, his tobacco, his chair.
The woman of the house a flash, a beam, a ticking
clock she hides beneath her dress.

She turns one book askew. He wants
the paper and then a paradox so she puts on
some music. He gets a little kick from his glass.

Stains settle on the floral sofa. Above the mantle
she hangs a painting, a house, like the model one
she lives inside. Its ivy-covered walls keep what's out

out, what's in in. The bedroom waits upstairs
but when she's in it everything goes white
in unspeakableness. A person comes in her body

and the walls are amnesiac white. Up and down
the stairs she goes. Up, around. Descends, descends.
The shadows of the lamp are throats.

The husband finds she no longer lies beside him.
The husband knows what he did.
Holding her neck, the doctor turns her head.

He faces her toward the living room
so she can see the mess the man has made.
The telephone rings and rings on the floor.

2.

THE COURT OF NO RECORD

When I leap, I briefly see
the world as it is and as it should be.

—CORNELIUS EADY, "Jazz Dancer"

IN THE COURT OF NO RECORD

Broken Mirror County

THE ALPHA,
     Petitioner,

vs.

████████████████████,
     Respondent.

Case No. ████████
████

and

THE ALPHA,
     Petitioner,

vs.

████████████████████,
     Respondent.

Case No. ████████

TRANSCRIPT OF PROCEEDINGS

BE IT REMEMBERED that the above-captioned cause came on for hearing, on this, the 24th day of November, 2019, wherein two victims of emotional, verbal, and physical abuse by the hand of THE ALPHA were brought to court in BROKEN MIRROR COUNTY before the HONORABLE ANSWER. The respondents will spend $████████ in legal and travel fees defending themselves from their abuser, on account of alleged breaking of silence, for speaking and writing about the abuse, when and where the following proceedings were had, to wit:

For the Respondents:
     ATTORNEY A
For the Petitioner:
     ATTORNEY B

PROCEEDINGS

The Honorable Answer offers me the option to reset my court date due to his personal relationship with my abuser's mother. I have driven halfway across middle Unmerica, through rhinestone-studded stampedes and the great dripping caves of the Bible Belt, to Broken Mirror County. Broken Mirror, where I was once thrown in a room with a pit bull. The dog slept with his sweet paw around me and breathed his panicky breath into my neck. To say *me* is a stretch—the self was a rock blown into many rocks, sparkling and hot. The Alpha made of me a souvenir. He put me in a box he occasionally opened, then vanished me in the palm of his hand.

Whereupon, the following proceedings are heard in the Court of No Record, to say *heard* is a stretch. To say *stretch* is a lie. My pleated pants are drenched in sweat as my abuser's lawyer, in her wrinkled skirt and ruffled sweater, heckles me into a corner. To say *corner* is generous, because in the Court of No Record, where the abuser is petitioner and the victim respondent, the walls are made of ideas, so the men can walk straight through them.

Briefly, your Honor. Thou shalt not bring the hire of a whore, or the price of a dog, into the house of God for any vow: for even both these are abomination unto the LORD thy God.[1] This is what the LORD says: In the place where dogs licked up the Alpha's blood, dogs will lick up your blood—yes, yours![2] For dogs have surrounded him; the congregation of the wicked has enclosed him. They pierced his hands and feet.[3] She that killeth an ox is as if she slew a man; she that sacrificeth a lamb, as if she cut off a dog's neck; she that offereth an oblation, as if she offered swine's blood; she that burneth incense, as if she blessed an idol. Yea, they have chosen their own ways, and their souls delighteth in their abominations.[4]

1. Deuteronomy 23:18
2. 1 Kings 21:19
3. Psalm 22:16
4. Isaiah 66:3

THE VICTIMS' ATTORNEY:
OPENING STATEMENT

In my ten years of practice I have never seen such . . . In my ten years of practice I have never felt such . . . Here is a boy with a bat in his hand. I am no vehicle for false light, hand over a bulb that glows its own blood.

Honorable Answer, perjury will be committed today. My clients are muzzled. My clients are victims. I must speak on their behalf. I must read, highlight, and underline them. The petitioner will make a sparkling dogma of his victimhood. His pain is real. Their pain is real. I must encourage you to see their story as truth.

These four corners of the court hearing's statutes are the earth's four corners: threat, harassment, fright, alarm. My clients know no cardinal direction. Flip the invention of the petitioner's world. Reveal the red of truth. My clients have traveled far. They are weary. You will not hear them.

THE HONORABLE ANSWER SPEAKS

I know you are very zealous. I appreciate that. Please, let me rule? Pardon me while I unveil my friendship with the abuser's mother. Pardon me while I cite my expertise on domestic abuse. Pardon me while I eat this bag of Cheez-Its for I have missed my lunch. Pardon me while I do not hear. Pardon my confusion about the internet. Pardon me, but some abusers can be very sad. Pardon me but a person can feel harassed. Pardon me but why don't these women stand up for themselves? Pardon me but a victim of abuse must bear the weight of paperwork. Pardon me but have you tried the police? There is help for you if you prove your case. If you go through the proper channels. If you humiliate yourself. You place your body in harm. You stand before the court in proper attire. You endure the long hours. You return home under the law, protected by a signature. And the threat of police. Who may or may not respond. Who may or may not respond violently. Who may or may not come.

EVIDENCE

Her thighs—
out of nowhere,
purple blossoms surfaced.
Eruptions, as if no one had
struck her.

TESTIMONY OF THE ALPHA

Please rise. Please sit. Yes I loved these dogs. The second was better than the first, who is a busted hag-dog. The first bared her hag teeth and her saliva fell over everything. I carried the hag-dog by the neck until she could not speak. I filed these papers because despite my teeth she keeps barking. The second dog was hysterical. The second was more like a cat, now that I think about it. A cat's large green eyes are liars. The hag captured the cat. The hag turned her familiar. Twitter is very mean. People are very mean when they repeat the things you did to them. The hag and the cat have a plan. I am not very good at understanding this thing called gas lighting but I think it comes from a movie.

EVIDENCE: SHE SAID

Books flew
from his rage: bird
plague. His voice a siren,
mercy an expense I couldn't
afford.

STATEMENT OF THE ALPHA'S ATTORNEY

I say unto thee, these women belong to a cult against men. For a whore is a deep ditch; and a strange woman is a narrow pit.[1] My client dreams of the respondents. They spew the blood spatter of men. They awaken my client. They *unsettle* my client.

I submit to the evidence, your Honor, a copy of their manifesto, which calls for the murder of all men. Despite contradictory evidence, I submit that these women are the manifesto's authors. Draw near hither, ye sons of the sorceress, the seed of the adulterer and the whore.[2] You shall know about your mothers, who plot your fathers' death.

1. Proverbs 23:27
2. Isaiah 57:3

EVIDENCE: HE SAID

The beach.
A dusk became
me. Next thing, a star fell.
Her limbs and head its five points. Small
black hole.

CROSS-EXAMINATION OF THE ALPHA

—Are you racist, sir?—Excuse me? Well I think there was an exchange, sir, about white culture and basketball, that we—what exactly did we say?—It was a white player, sir—someone called him a Nazi. He said, *Don't put it in my face that being a white guy is something I'm supposed to be ashamed of, I'm proud of who I am.*—Are you proud of who you are, sir?—Well she called him a Nazi, and I'm white, sir. I'm not ashamed. I'm proud. As we all should be.—Are you sure, sir?—And I found it disturbing, and didn't really understand what was wrong with—they said—white people have no culture, which isn't true.—Did you write this, sir?—I call it art, sir. Art is allowed to be offensive. She said lots of negative things about white people, which is really hurtful, sir, because I am a white man. And I would say, stop being so mean to white people.—And then, after you said—I didn't say the word, I wrote it. It is art, sir.—Objection, relevance, whether or not he is publicly racist plays no part in this order of protection. He has been personally harmed.—She made them think I'm racist, sir, for things I said in private! They're taking an opportunity to stick it to a white man, sir. It is my race and sex and assumed gender, sir, that are getting in the way, not me specifically. I wouldn't consider anything I'm saying to be particularly racist. And additionally, sir, research has shown that pretty much everyone is racist. I'm a little taken aback, sir, with the idea that white people should be ashamed of being white.

EVIDENCE: HE SAID

Those men
are worse than me.
Red mufflers blast roads raw.
Even hit their wives. Impulse? I
curb it.

REDIRECT EXAMINATION BY THE
ALPHA'S ATTORNEY

The MeToo poem was shocking, was it not? This was her dogged power of persuasion and not your actions, correct? The accused has written a poem about your treatment of her, has she not? And the poem, though it does not name you, leads people to believe you are the abuser because the whole world is watching, correct? She takes your private statements wildly out of context in this poem that details her experience with "abuse," does she not? Though you did none of these things, you recognize yourself in the poem, correct? You are baffled, are you not, to have been MeToo-ed? This causes you great emotional and professional harm, yes? Her poems exceed the boundary of creative expression, yes? And the other woman, she affirmed the false claims of this poet, did she not? She is a liar too, is she not? And all the other women, liars as well, correct?

EVIDENCE: HE SAID

I taped
to her mirror
a note. *He thinks I am*
beautiful. She ripped it. The bitch
ripped me.

RECESS IN BROKEN MIRROR COUNTY

What kind of school is this? Two little girls attend the hearing. We take a recess and the children play in the courtyard. The girls had heard of their cousin's cruelty, his sexual assault. The girls are chatter birds on a wire, feathers oiled. They twitter back at us: *liar, liar.* Only a few birds will rape: ducks, egrets, bee-eaters. The girls hang upside down, small feet clutching. Flighty necks twitch to see the world from his angle. If I could go back in time and teach myself distrust, I would. If I could do it for them, I would. If I could walk backwards from this courthouse and into my life.

At security a man sifts through my purse with a stick. He pecks with his hand until my stomach opens: little love notes, chewing gum, my careful breakfast exposed. When he is done, he replaces my beating liver, my insubordinate heart.

The sky is strangulation blue. The November air says I belong to the earth and not the court. *Guard your heart,* a poet friend tells me. *By abiding with those who have not been accompanied by our systems of justice, you are on the side of the angels.* The newly planted lacebark elms whisper the court's atrocities. They push through their concrete dividers. The child of me held by security at the gate.

EVIDENCE: SHE SAID

The cops?
When he chased me
down an alley, they stood
blue, unmoved. He can spin a badge.
Turn them.

MY TESTIMONY

My name is called. I walk to the witness stand. The eyes in the courtroom on my back. (Even my hair feels stupid. I am back in the prison of the Alpha.) He laughs at me. (I try not to feel it on my face, like a virus come in through the blood.) "You are well aware of why you're here." (I want to shout, to run, to set the building on fire.) But in the Court of No Record, you cannot react. I sit with my hands in my lap.

"Tell us about your tumultuous relationship. Tell us of your arguments." (Many things I cannot speak.) "We didn't argue," I say, "he abused me, verbally and emotionally, for hours on end." (I didn't know if I existed, either.) "But you aren't here as the victim," his lawyer says. I say nothing. "Exactly," the judge says.

"I don't need to know whether these things happened to her," the judge says, "only if she wrote about them." (I sweat. I look at my friend.) I look at my friend (who says with her mind: *You know who you are. You know who you are.*)

"Do you understand this would be humiliating to him?" the attorney asks. "Do you stand by what you said of him?" the Honorable Answer asks. I'm sorry, your Honor, I say. Let me explain, your Honor. "It's a yes or no question," he says. Yes, I say. I do. (I do.)

EVIDENCE: SHE SAID

I wear
chartreuse. Under-
eye bags. People whisper.
I heard she made it up. See me,
then don't.

HER TESTIMONY

I let go of her hand, turning blue. We have been in court eight hours. (Between our hearts, a tether, a leash.) When she cries, I cry. (A doggy sound, a cat too high in a tree. Curled about the night from the inside out.) When she describes her abuse, the lawyer says, "Again, your Honor, not relevant, you Honor." At the plaintiff's table, laughter erupts. "Was there coerced sex in your relationship?" the lawyer asks. "Yes," she says. "We are killing a lot of trees," the lawyer says, handing over the evidence. (I channel my night vision, pitch its green across the room.) The Honorable Answer says, "You must understand that sometimes people are in different phases of their journey with abuse." (I am strapped to my chair. I bark from the forest floor. I disappear the wooden witness stand.) The court does not care. (The court will open the wound, will fill it with paper.)

EVIDENCE: SHE SAID

Poor trees.
When he'd go out
howling, they'd stand tongue-tied
as he spread his body's splutter
on bark.

CLOSING STATEMENT OF THE
ALPHA'S ATTORNEY

Therefore the showers have been withholden, and there hath been no latter rain; and thou hadst a whore's forehead, thou refusedst to be ashamed.[1]

This is a cycle. We must silence these women for my client's sake. I warn the fathers of this room: Do not prostitute thy daughter, to cause her to be a whore; lest the land fall to whoredom, and the land become full of wickedness.[2] I recommend that you punish these women, your Honor.

And you, you women who harass with your stories, stalking the bedrooms of your abusers, I say: bring out the damsel to the door of her father's house, and the men of her city shall stone her with stones that she die: because she hath wrought folly in Broken Mirror, to play the whore in her father's house: so shalt thou put evil away from among you.[3]

1. Jeremiah 3:3
2. Leviticus 19:29
3. Deuteronomy 22:21

OUR ATTORNEY'S CLOSING STATEMENT

We have what we call, in the study of law, an eggshell plaintiff, susceptible to his feelings. Under the four corners of the statute, we must prove that a reasonable person feels threatened. We have not proven anything reasonable here today.

Evidence has been erased. How are reasonable people, like my clients, supposed to know when they're being lied to, baited? This is a fabrication brought upon the Court, you Honor. Your Honor has the power to judge the credibility of these women. I believe what they've told you. They believe what they've told you. I know you have an extensive background in domestic violence, your Honor. I don't think you're going to say that these women are lying, because nothing they've said has been disputed. Perception is in the eye of the beholder. To a hammer, everything looks like a nail. It's got to be anything but the hammer, he thinks. Not me, he thinks.

At the end of the day, people are allowed to express themselves. That's the First Amendment. And I think what they're doing is okay. It is art. What is art? An expression of life, our tribulations. It's scary. Maybe people like it, maybe they don't. Maybe they relate, maybe they don't. What's terrifying, what's terrifying to me is that to this hammer, everything in his future will look like a nail.

THE HONORABLE ANSWER SENTENCES

Sir, because I cannot prove whether or not you abused these women, and I cannot prove whether or not this woman caused you to lose anything in your life, you are in the wrong court. For the other woman, though, I have some issues. You, ma'am, are an advocate. Your job is to advocate for other people, correct, for unions? You have your own truths, okay, and I'm not saying it's not the truth. But when you're trying to help what I would call domestic violence, you have to be very careful because you don't know where people are or whether they're in safe spaces. If they want your help, they will ask for it. I am troubled by your truth-telling. How loud it is. How vocal. This speaking out has caused this man emotional distress. So I will grant the order of protection here. Ma'am, do you own or possess a gun? During this year you cannot own or possess a gun. Please stay to sign the papers.

3.

WHAT LOVE DOES

After a while I understand that,
talking this way, everything dissolves: *justice,
pine, hair, woman, you,* and *I.*

—ROBERT HASS, "Meditation at Lagunitas"

BITCH INTERRUPTS A WEDDING

A black and blue pipevine butterfly
noses the collars of orange zinnias—something

someone might write a poem about,
someone who isn't a bitter bitch, or mostly likely a man

with nothing else to do but splooge his sensitive musings
down a sentence paved with fancy names

for insects or plants or birds—*O swoon, red-banded
hairstreak butterfly, O sigh and hark the yonder Black-Eyed*

*Susans, the rudbeckia subtomentosa,
the night hawk and dickcissel*—and I stop by

the cave trickle of a natural spring where air is cold
as a winter tongue or Cailleach's outstretched hand

or some bullshit, side-stepping the bikers who have stopped
to smooch in the grotto, my hand over my mouth because I have forgotten

my mask, so that now, ambling down the charming Victorian
Ozarkian streets I appear to be in a constant state of shock,

gasping into my own hand, and actually, I am in a constant state
of shock, as I had long ago decided that the universe

could only really push a person so far, that, if there was no God,
at least the world possessed a kind of omniscient fairness,

a cosmic balance, trees leaning into wind, meaning in the goo
of the chrysalis that turns to prismatic wings,

and with the one hand over my mouth and the other
on the hiking trail railing to guide my arthritic knee

I think, at least there's this lovely respite, gazing
onto the green and dappled light

as forty unmasked faces, weird little forest moons,
crank upwards—an ivory dress, and bridesmaid blue,

fall flowers and pews and an aisle, and I hear the minister
saying *and now I pronounce you* as the bride in her sparkling

white lace waits patiently for this bitch to stop ruining the moment
her life will begin forever and I blubber back up the stairs

picking a piece of mossy bark from my ponytail
and the sun prisms my arms and a passing hawk

darkens the afternoon for just a moment,
and I am young, and I am breathing, and,

praise Ozark Jesus, I am the interruption
and not the wanted moment that will pass.

JENNY | JENNIFER: SONOGRAM

At fakeababy.com, you can get a personalized sonogram,
pregnancy papers, a glucose count.

Jennifer went to the 24-hour computer lab,
printed an ultrasound photo,

and signed her name in its insomniac scrawl,
craggy across the straight line the computer made.

Then she drove to the frat house. Its white stucco mouth
spit out Trey in his football t-shirt.

Maybe he would give her a little money. Maybe if she
thought hard enough, he could love her.

The sun set fat and sweaty
before the giant dorm windows.

The rec center was an institution on fire.
The harvest moon swung up over the lake

alive with snaky tails of nutria.
Jennifer, don't go in.

Jennifer, try to sleep.
I too went crazy over an ultrasound.

They searched not for a heartbeat but a tumor,
the screen over my head

showing me my insides. What destroys me
must also make a sound.

At the dorm, Jennifer sat in her red vest on the back stoop,
the crumpled photo print in her pocket, teeth

like fireflies behind her curtain of smoke.
What's the difference between love and force? I cannot tell.

BITCH AS SHEEPDOG

Before shearing the sheepfold
sleeps and the singular dodgy eyes

dart like wolfish hands
under a blanket. This

marriage bed. Once I lost another
dog. Once I lost them both.

At night I think of anyone
but him. I begin to notice

how he hates my questions.
I move to feed the animals.

The little one licks the bowl.
The bigger one squeezes me

around the ribs until I cannot
breathe. And the wolf—

I catch him staring
when I am quiet,

as if he'd unstitch my skin, too,
and open my head, hardwire

my brain into submission.
Even after he kills me,

he puts his ear to the coarse
pastoral of my shame. Trembly

voice. The pelts at his feet.
By his works he should be known.

THE POOL

The Elms Hotel, Excelsior Springs, Missouri

We no longer believe
in the healing power of the water.
Iron. Manganese.

But a girl was cured
of tuberculosis here. Opal.
Meaning, she reflected light.

Luminous and inviolable, Opal.
The water left rust on limestone,
liquid gold. Her lung-shadows

disappeared into the pools.
I once saw my own ghost. I tell you this
as the Elms's underground pool

splashes in the hotel bowels
with no one in it. My therapist
drew two bubbles,

one swelling, flooding
the other, and said, *these are your thoughts.*
You must contain them.

What are the laws of my body?
I contain spirit which a spirit
can pass through. Short of breath,

I buzz. Or I am a bag
of water and something
called thought.

The ghost I once saw in Dallas
was one of my unhealthy thoughts
because she was a part of me,

a future of me, the ghost of a child
I would not have. She looked
not through me but into me.

There is no one at the pool,
but you don't have to prove
a ghost story, that's the point.

The paranormal tour guide
says there is a child who lives in this water,
that her footprints never dry.

No one wants me, not really.
Out here, the woods are electrified
by lightning storms.

The chandeliers quake.
A woman can be heard
singing through the walls.

I am untouchable.
I wake to too much stillness.
No current, no charge, just swelling.

I shake you awake—*the power's out*—
You turn on the light.
A girl floods the room.

JENNY | JENNIFER: ARIES SEASON

Jennifer was the part of me on fire.
I'd gone to the bars, Amaretto sours

then some older man's hot tub, who,
that night, I avoided. It happened slowly

with Jennifer—the frogs sung us faded—
then I knew her, her mother's last pack

of cigarettes, the hard Atlantic
of her face. I went to class and Jennifer

stayed back in her tiger-striped pajamas,
hair going matted. She slept for days.

Something turned, some sever, some
wedge, then she passed me in the halls

cursing under her breath, the flyered walls
closing in. The elevator beeped like a broken

smoke detector. My meal pass a dog tag,
my hunger dressed in a cotton skirt.

I stopped beginning and she stopped ending
and plexiglass erected around us until we were both

the mascot in a cage by the stadium.
You think you're a good person, she said one day.

I'm giving her reasons to live. For myself,
a question, a parallel universe. That night

I came back to the dorm and my door
was on the floor. The RA checked my ID;

I knew I'd done something wrong
but couldn't remember what.

My lock clattered around like wind-up
teeth on the concrete floor.

Jennifer needed me to know she existed.
Jennifer existed. I didn't understand.

The next day she was gone. Someone came
to clear out her room, her Hole poster,

her homework all done. I didn't know what else to do
so I walked to class. I stepped in the shadows

the dogwood made on the path, the sweat bare
as spring on my back, the branches striping my legs.

LATE TO THE PARTY

The person I can't marry
says he feels *late to the party*.
I conjure the party of my twenties—
a man's jealous rage, my back against
cinderblock, salsa, mescal. The end of a child.
Zipping myself in a tent at the dumb music festival.
A tattoo meant to excise some adolescent pain.
He was married young, a Marine, believes
fun is honest, which is one of the reasons
I try to make it sound like I was happy.
I am a hopeful person, even in past tense.
Even in tonight's dream—
naked or half-naked, covered in soap,
partygoers laughing as I rearrange
my fallen bra, try not to touch my face.
My fiancé flirts with someone younger,
someone more beautiful. I say aloud
to no one, *I am going to be fine.*
I say this with conviction, almost believing it,
as the people turn away, embarrassed.
Needing to run, I look for my dog,
who I am supposed to keep alive,
who waited for me for fourteen years
in a dark apartment. I call and call her name
but a circle has formed. They wear scrubs,
they intubate us both. She blinks her one
remaining eye at me, then slinks into sleep.
The people go home, even my fiancé
and his new girl. I remain at the party
with a tube in my throat, steps littered
in dregs of celebration (crumbed plates,
empty bottles, ashes on the ground).

YOU'RE JUST LIKE EVERYONE ELSE

He'll say anything He'll make a steamboat of his mouth
and out comes a sick green river *You're the only one*

You're water and oar You're wind
and undertow *We'll fuck until we fly*

You know what he'll do *You're just like everyone else*
He only says this to you You're his only one

He beautifies the yard Trashed bottle caps on nails
A tin can for every splinter You'll one day

give him sons A cat sleeps in the car The birds
know better He has ten tempers Each one

an incubus Your mirror is the wrong painting
Mornings you wake as no one

He is easy to believe *He thinks I'm beautiful*
He says *You're beautiful* You are someone

who reads the rage language This is the dance
The underwater dance and you're the only one

These are the steps to the dance
This is the music *You're just like everyone*

else in this world The worst thing to be—
no one and anyone

in a world full of someones like him
You twirl pretty until it's true You're no one

Then he pins you down Fills your mouth
with salt Your flaws Every faulty one

You're packed like a buried fish
You cure for winter You even sleep for once

You like the mirror the sun makes of water
Like being alive You're done

You slip down drains You love your own scales
You hate getting caught Like everyone else

THE NEW HOSPITAL

> Wrongness came like a lone finger / chopping through the
> room and he ducked. What was that? said one of the others /
> turning toward him centuries later.
>   —ANNE CARSON, *Autobiography of Red*

My father walks
through the hall of blood.

Dreamed from inside
the earth. Body materials.

A wall formed. Detachment.
Wings full of holes.

I swear an uncontained object
opened out of the body.

Cardinals a red flash.
Ways to find blood:

Luminol. Holy wings. Someone
you once thought out of fire.

What are the most important questions:
The great mystery, the fact

of empathy, talking to her
like a child. What if I ended it.

Woman's work
until metal is softened.

After he is gone, something splits.
Myoglobin gene, secret language.

Wonder like a limb.
I start to see his lack

of remorse. Whole blood
forever redirecting

the topographical brain.
Cost and potential

failure. I swear, opened out of—
this makes me angry—out of shame.

BITCH MONITORING YOUR PHONE

I am a citizen detective. I am a sleuth.
Now that I know where you are, I do not care.

What shall I call my wave-colored moon?
How will I occupy it? Where will I erect my flag?

The blue tracker dot waits in the red traffic.
Don't come near me, little blue dot.

May every sad woman see herself in a mirror.
May she see, may she believe what she sees.

I was too afraid to see that I have always been brave.

WHAT THE FOREST DOES

I decided to let them take the eye.
The only ethical exorcism—a softer failure.
All the court needed to convict was my woman's
body, my required head. I put my hand over the eye:
> *I'm not sure I've a good mind.*
> *I'm not sure I reason well.*
How weak the man-made earth about softness,
about quiet. Depression a vaseline gloss on the lens.
Propensities do not form ideas. She still flinches, turns
her head to the dark side of my usually burning urge.
Against the green berried needles, the frontal view,
compromising. My partner counting seeds: tall
pink hollyhock. Showy milkweed. Queen Anne's Lace.
Behind plastic windows, the body in bed. Feelings
arise without functioning. I cannot work, one eye
still looking out. Still looking at me. The one eye.
I felt like picturing myself, even in the dark.

AGAINST "THE DOVER BITCH"

after Anthony Hecht

Once I read *a fairly good translation* of Hesiod
and this girl who was me slithered along the spine,
deferential to the men who keep the poetry.
As my daddy said, I've cussed between the lines.
You *musn't judge* me *by that*. I've many heads.
I speak to suit the rooms they move in.
Xenic breath. In each a brain, *running to fat*.
Though I respect a man's regarded work,
Shakespearean allusions, American
remembrances of a horrible war, when you show me
a good time, you only make me smarter.
I do recall that day on shore, your basket of beer
and French perfume, how you pinched
my waist and laughed, your wife none the wiser.
I feel you on my neck, my many necks.
You double-occupy me: the cliffs of Dover
at my back, the mighty empire fallen, and me a girl—
my heady, flicking tongue, overly sweet, my dependable anger
your oyster. Once at a dive, I watched an old man run
his hands over the belly of a beautiful woman,
pregnant the fifth time, then admire her heels
as she clicked away, no choice but to let him touch her.
I'm *really all right*. I smell with my mouth.
Lilacs, bread, a grandpa's musty breath. I know,
I know, you're angry. You also took me to be yours.

BITCH UNDER A TREE EATING WENDY'S

The pine tree and I give each other breath
but if I'm honest I only give so many fucks
about the pine tree, and it gives zero about me.

The pine tree lets somebody else do its fucking.
I can get behind that. When people walk by I scowl
and bend deeper into my spicy chicken sandwich.

I can't do kissing right. I get so aware of a person
climbing inside my body which for so long
I've been trying to protect. People say, please don't

shut down, but I've been noticing the perfect
golden yellow of this fry wearing its backdrop of grass.
If you look at grass under a microscope, smiley faces

bedevil its cells. A bitch's body is an oven full
of sweets but a bitch is not a witch; she's emptier
when they're gone. I can't do love right.

I keep thinking, I'm a fat bitch, which is egocentric.
Some love is a capitalist exchange: open slit,
a pig's back. Bitches get tired of being all hole.

AGAINST THE CULT OF TRUE WOMANHOOD

They are only semi-women, mental hermaphrodites . . .
—HENRY F. HARRINGTON, on suffragettes, in the
Ladies' Companion, 1838

"It is not the custom to employ females!" the man
of the story exclaims like a broken parrot.
Kate Warne, 23, America's first female detective.
Kate my talisman as I drive to court to face my abuser
for the third time. It's 1856. Or it's 2019. Kate foxes
her way into high secessionist society, dressed
as a fine southern lady, champagne flute an appendage,
fleur-de-lis pin glinting with impending war. The men flirt
with their gold-plated pistols. Kate's eye stenographs
the folds of a flag, the violining of fly legs on a corpse,
the slave-trader's side-eye behind his canteen.
Enigma Kate, AKA Kitty Warren, Kay Warner, Mrs. Barley,
Mrs. Cherry—even her gravestone misspelled: WARN.
A mayday. Kate, a reminder that even a woman
who saves the President must shut up.

     *

On a train from Harrisburg to Baltimore, Kate Warne
dresses Abraham Lincoln in a shawl and a soft felt cap.
He poses as an invalid while she never sleeps,
her blue eye an invisible searchlight. She plays
rich woman, Mrs. Secessionist, purveyor of all things
ruined with charm. Sometimes I take a plane
to go to court, sometimes I drive. This goes on
for months, the judge's dismissal, the man's appeal,
my poems shoved in the hands of lawyers, a judge
lowering her glasses, a judge shaking her head, a judge
finding the better language with which to excuse me.

The man says I killed his baby. I'd never been pregnant.
The man's face purples on the bench. I speak of how
I hid for three years, forcing my shaking hands between my thighs,
how I was afraid to sleep or bathe. I must submit
even to the destruction of my own body. Now on the train
the Western front is quiet. Stars like splatters of luminol
against the sky's black floor. The judges have finally
purged my record, my poems tucked back in a book.
But when the silence rumbles, thuds of a man's footsteps
throb down the hallway, and when I lower my spyglass,
a stain darkens my clothes.

ACKNOWLEDGMENTS

I am deeply grateful to the following friends, writers, and editors who read or published earlier drafts of these poems, supported my work, and inspire me in their love of the craft: Erin Adair-Hodges, Ruth Awad, Taneum Bambrick, Hadara Bar-Nadav, F. Douglas Brown, Leila Chatti, Nicole Cooley, Caitlin Cowan, Kyle Dargan, Denise Duhamel, K.K. Fox, Tanya Grae, Christian Gullette, Danielle Holland, Peter LaBerge, Bridget Lowe, Shara McCallum, Jennifer Maritza McCauley, Marc McKee, Philip Metres (quoted in "Recess in Broken Mirror County"), Wayne Miller, Ron Mitchell, Caridad Moro, Kathryn Nuernberger, Heidi Seaborn, Lauren Slaughter, Adam Vines, and Hananah Zaheer.

A special thank you to David Keplinger, forever my champion, teacher, and friend. To Puja Datta, my hero, my twin soul. And to Jonny Ulasien, my whole heart, for unending support, kindness, enthusiasm, and love.

Thank you to Nathan, a.k.a. Nicky Slish, for seeing through it, and seeing us through.

Many thanks to the Writer's Colony at Dairy Hollow and the Longleaf Writers Conference for the gift of time and space, and to the editors at LSU Press, for their important work, and for believing in this book.

Thank you to the editors of the following journals for originally publishing these poems:

The Account: "Closing Statement of the Alpha's Attorney," "Evidence," "Our Attorney's Closing Statement," and "The Honorable Answer Sentences"; *AGNI:* "Bitch Under a Tree Eating Wendy's"; *The Adroit Journal:* "Baton Rouge, Harvest Moon," "Occam's Razor," "Runaway," and "Proceedings"; *Bear Review:* "Trigger"; *Birmingham Poetry Review:* "My Testimony," "The

Living Room," and "Against 'The Dover Bitch'"; *Copper Nickel:* "Hunting"; *The Cortland Review:* "The Pool" and "The New Hospital"; *Couplet Poetry:* "Testimony of the Alpha" and "Her Testimony"; *Crazyhorse:* "Jenny | Jennifer: Sonogram"; *Diode:* "The Victims' Attorney: Opening Statement" and "The Honorable Answer Speaks"; *Gulf Stream:* "The Alpha's Attorney: Opening Statement," "Bitch Monitoring Your Phone," "Bridge," "Evidence: He Said [The beach]," "Evidence: She Said [The cops]," "Evidence: She Said [I wear]," "Examination by the Alpha's Attorney," "Redirect," "Shooting at Oakbrook Apartments," "Statement of the Alpha's Attorney," and "You're Just Like Everyone Else." *Kansas City Poetry Anthology* (Woodneath Press): "Against the Cult of True Womanhood"; *Memorious:* "My Scorpion" and "Bitch as Sheepdog"; *The Missouri Review:* "Bitch Interrupts a Wedding"; *NELLE:* "Collisions"; *Ploughshares:* "Recess in the Court of No Record"; *Poetry Northwest:* "Expecting" and "Late to the Party"; *The Seventh Wave:* "May the Stars Guide You Safely Home," "Attic," "The Pink Bathroom," and "A Joke"; *South Carolina Review:* "Initiation in White" and "Jenny | Jennifer : Aries Season"; *Southern Indiana Review:* "Family with the Dreams Cut Out"; *Verse Daily:* "Against 'The Dover Bitch" and "Family with Dreams Cut Out"; and *West Branch:* "The Miniaturist."

NOTES

"The Pink Bathroom," "Attic," "The Miniaturist," and "The Living Room" are written in response to Corrine Botz's photographs of Frances Glessner Lee's miniature crime scenes that were displayed at Harvard University for police crime scene investigation study.

"Collisions" is inspired by the form in C.D. Wright's poem "The Night I Met Little Floyd."

Details from "Bridge" are taken from *Dismembered,* by Susan D. Mustafa and Sue Israel.

"Cross-Examination of the Alpha" takes cues from the anaphora in "Aaron Bur, Sir," from Lin-Manuel Miranda's *Hamilton.*

The italicized lines in "What the Forest Does" are taken from Maggie Nelson's *Jane: A Murder.*

"Against 'The Dover Bitch'" is a response to Anthony Hecht's poem "The Dover Bitch." Italicized lines are taken from the original poem.

"Against the Cult of True Womanhood" is inspired by *The Pinks: The First Women Detectives, Operatives, and Spies with the Pinkerton National Detective Agency,* by Chris Enss.

Printed in the USA
CPSIA information can be obtained
at www.ICGtesting.com
CBHW031323150524
8605CB00002B/63

9 780807 179024